Your Next Thought

Your Next Thought

Robert Paradiso

Copyright © 2020 Robert Paradiso

Cover Photo Credit:
"Coney Island Sunset" by Patrick Tappe/Shutterstock.com

All rights reserved.

Disclaimers:
I have tried to recreate events and conversations from my memories of them. But as I mention in this book we don't always choose what we remember.

I've referred to several people in this book simply as "my friend" to protect their privacy. But those present at the events recounted will know who they are.

This book is not intended as professional advice or counseling of any sort. I'm just a guy who looked closely at life for a while and thinks he saw something. For those curious what they too might find, I provide here some things to try. But the final decision to do so and its results are yours.

First paperback edition May 2020

ISBN 978-1-7347774-0-6 (paperback)
ISBN 978-1-7347774-1-3 (e-book)

Robert Paradiso
https://bobparadiso.com/
bobparadiso@gmail.com
.

CONTENTS

1 | Introduction...1

2 | Backstory..5

3 | Who...13

4 | Punishment...27

5 | Calm...41

6 | Flow...55

7 | New Beginnings.....................................71

8 | Tools...79

Closing...93

Reading List...95

1 | Introduction

Growing up, home was not a place where I felt safe. My dad was physically and verbally abusive to both my brother and I over the course of many years. In this book I share part of that story and others from my life since then. Some of these stories were painful to relive as I wrote them. Some are embarrassing to now have in print. But there was something that I needed to explain, and these stories afforded me a way to do that.

This book attempts to draw your attention to a core part of being human. Although usually either unnoticed or misunderstood, it influences everything we do and colors everything we experience. One way to shine a light on it is to seriously consider the following question: Do you consciously choose your next thought?

An incredible amount rides on how you answer that question. I'm not asking here if your next thought comes from within or outside of you, where that line is, or if it exists. Regardless of that the question is: Do you consciously choose each thought that comes to you? Do you deliberate over what your next thought should be, or consider all the possible next thoughts you could have? To consider or evaluate would itself require more thoughts, how would those be chosen?

These are not questions to pose to scientists or religious authorities. They are questions for *you*, about your own direct experience. You can, and I believe must, see the answers for yourself. From your perspective, looking through the window of your consciousness, does your next thought just pop up for you? Perhaps, as far as you can directly experience, thoughts and emotions just arise in your mind. Maybe you hear them, or they come into view. Maybe at times you feel them, or you just get the sense of them. In whatever form your thoughts come to you, do you ask for them or do they just appear? Please, take some time now to check this out for yourself.

Could it be that you don't choose your thoughts, and by extension the actions those thoughts motivate? Look at your reaction there and figure out to what degree you chose it. Whatever thoughts or feelings came up, whether for or against, emotional or intellectual, did you choose for each of them to come up? Can you catch a glimpse of your thoughts and feelings in the process of arising? Our view of this process is the foundation of how we assign blame. We blame people for the choices they make.

That blame justifies and fuels the overt and subtle ways we punish ourselves and others. But our view of all this can instead inform how to best help those same people. There is freedom and power in understanding the constraints of one's situation. In seeing and empathizing with our common human situation, there can be deeper understanding and connection.

These pages are a guided exploration into how our mind works, blame and its consequences, and how to pause and choose a different course. I present stories from my life and some exercises to facilitate this exploration. All too often we punish ourselves and others, causing more harm than benefit. My aim with this book is to point towards a better way, and as a result, help our inner and outer worlds become a friendlier place to live.

2 | Backstory

It feels like a lifetime ago that my dad was still alive. He died when I was fifteen, the same age he was when his dad died. I'll call him "dad" even though he once sternly corrected me: "We don't have that kind of relationship. I'm your 'father'." By that point there wasn't any warmth between us. For many years he had been the enforcer; and he was always the "king." I was constantly on edge around him, and even more so in the last few years of his life after he started to lose his mind.

My younger brother and I had learned to fear his anger early on. His primary method of discipline was whipping us with his leather belt. When it was time, he would bark at me to "Drop 'em and bend over!" I would stand there, bent over, pants and underwear around my ankles. He would pull off his belt and crack it a few times as I fearfully anticipated that first lash against my skin. I never knew when he would hit me with the metal buckle end. Many times I would cry so hard that tears and mucus ran past my mouth.

He would also have us stand in a corner for long hours, sometimes right after being whipped. If we were in deep enough trouble, we would stand there through most of the night, even after he fell asleep. He usually chose the corner near his bedroom so he could keep an eye on us. We were not to lean against the wall, no matter how tired we became. If he noticed us touching the wall, we were hit and made to stand there longer. Food was scarce at times and I became prone to fainting. Sometimes I would wake up on the ground after fainting from the hours of standing. I would just get up again and continue. Eventually, during one of his bathroom trips, or at the end of a late-night movie, he would tell me to get out of his sight and I would hurry back to my room and collapse in bed.

He woke me up in the middle of the night once. Apparently I had wet the bed again, though I don't know if he knew before or after he woke me. He ordered me to take my clothes off and lie down in the bathtub. The bathtub was cold against my skin, though not as cold as the freezing water he hosed me off with from the shower head. Afterward, I was sobbing as I knelt naked beside the toilet. I rinsed out my underwear in it while he stood over me. More than any physical pain his punishments caused, the embarrassment and emotional pain was the most devastating. I felt utterly unloved and worthless.

When I would wet the bed, or upset my mom, forget what I was told, or have trouble with something he thought should come easily, I had failed him. And he was going to make sure I never would again. But despite his belt, standing in the corner, being thrown into walls, punched in the chest, kicked with his work boots, and all the verbal abuse, I *did* continue to fail him. After one of these failures, he said to me, "Someday you'll understand what it means to be the first born." Though in his eyes, I don't think I ever did.

I hated how things were, but I had accepted them and found a way to live with them. That is until he started losing his mind. At one point he made my brother lick the inside of a dirty toilet bowl plunger. He became delusional and would get furious about things that never happened. Being worried and hurt, I asked my mom if dad would still be mad about these crazy things after he got better. I wondered, if he died before getting better, would he hate me in heaven? I still wanted him to like me; he was my "dad." But now there was no way to try and keep him happy with me. Things seemed unfair before but at least somewhat predictable. Now I would often end up on his "shit list" for events that had only occurred in his mind.

His neurological problems started soon after a camping trip in Virginia. He said he had gotten some bug bites, and the same type of bull's-eye pattern rash that results from Lyme disease eventually appeared on his back. He had many seizures, including one that led to him crashing a car at the automobile repair shop where he worked. He wasn't injured, but they let him go after that. After trying again briefly at another repair shop, he had to retire altogether. He would often lose feeling and the use of his legs for hours or days at a time. With some time on his hands, and more trouble driving, he decided to buy a very nice bicycle. After a bad crash during his first ride he never got back on. He was losing everything so quickly: control over his body, his livelihood, his independence, and even his mind.

When he didn't have use of his legs, I would push him around in an office chair to get him to the bathroom. That old armless chair wasn't nearly as useful as a proper wheelchair. Sometimes he would fall out or he would lean funny and the chair would tip over. I wasn't always strong enough to make it work. Sometimes a wheel would get caught on a broken part of the aging floor. I would try for a long time to get it free, but eventually he would ask me to get him an empty Coke bottle so he could relieve himself.

One day I came home from school as usual, walked around our house to the back door, and opened it. Then I started down the stairs to the basement where we lived. I saw my dad standing in the kitchen trying to whip my brother with his belt. My brother was hiding behind my mom, and her body was absorbing the belt hits. She yelled to me to "Go tell Shirley!" I ran as fast as I could to Shirley's house just around the block. I rang the bell, still breathing heavy. She opened the door and asked me what was wrong. I just stood there panting. I couldn't say anything. But being out of breath wasn't the reason. I just couldn't say it. So she called the police. She had talked with my mom often enough to guess what type of thing would send me running there.

After that my mom and uncle moved my dad upstairs. We kept the only door down to the basement locked from our side. My dad was in bad shape. When I had seen him standing in the kitchen that last time, his legs were trembling and unsteady. The new arrangement had many problems, but at least we were physically safe from him. My dad's brother beat him up one day when he came home from work. He had caught my dad in the process of taking the hinges off the door. He wanted to get back downstairs, it was his home, and he saw it as his right. Many days, he would yell through the floorboards, cursing my mom terribly, since he was sure she was cheating on him. They would meet upstairs for breakfast some mornings; she still cared a lot about him. Eventually he convinced her to let him try living downstairs again.

It "worked" for a while. They agreed that he would leave disciplining my brother and I to my mom. For a few weeks, he was able to hold it together. But one day, while he was sitting on the toilet with the bathroom door open, I walked by and he quickly became angry. He yelled at me about doing something, but I didn't understand. Then he called me over to him. I recognized that tone of voice and knew he wanted to hit me. But I thought we were done with that. I was supposed to finally be safe now. I made a snap judgment that I could get away from him. He was still on the toilet, and his legs weren't great that day. For the first time in my life I ran away from his wrath. In the past it had always been inconceivable, certain suicide. He was always all-powerful in my mind. No one ever crossed him and got away with it for long. So I ran as hard as I could, trying to make as much distance on foot running as possible before he got to his truck. He yelled to me to come back, first angrily commanding, then with a note of pleading. Maybe he realized.

But I was already locked into my plan and going to get as far from there as I could. For a long time, I kept looking over my shoulder for his truck. All my life that truck had provoked fear in me. We would watch with dread as its tires rolled into our driveway after his days at work. When we knew we were in trouble we would wait and listen for its engine noise to stop. Then we would soon hear the truck door slam shut right before he walked down the driveway to come inside. At some point while running I finally felt pretty safe. I figured that even if he got into his truck, I had made enough distance that he wouldn't easily find me. But I didn't have a plan, any money, or a good place to go. So after many hours, I walked back home. When I got there, he was locked upstairs again and my mom was waiting for me downstairs. She said to me, "I knew that if you ran away something wasn't right. So I got him back upstairs. I'm sorry." She never asked me what happened.

My dad was angry and determined to regain control. Eventually, there was a court case about custody of my brother and I, and rights to the basement. I waited outside the courtroom with my grandmother and my brother. In the end, my dad lost and there was a restraining order. The story I heard was that it was actually going pretty well for him, until he started to lose it and go on and on about how he's the king and his children are his soldiers.

Still, my dad had nowhere to go, and he needed care. My mom had pleaded with the judge for the restraining order to only include the basement. He never came downstairs again. We did talk often, through that locked upstairs door. He asked me on many occasions to unlock it for him, which I never did. I didn't get to see him again until his funeral.

One morning when I was the only one downstairs, about to head to school, I heard a thud upstairs. It sounded very wrong. I just stood there listening, waiting. But there was no sound after that. I would be late for school soon. I ran out the door. At the end of the school day a priest from my church picked me up outside to tell me what happened. He brought me to my grandmother who was at our house with my brother, while my mom was still in the hospital with my dad. Later, my mom explained to me how she found him and how he must have had another one of his seizures and fell, hitting his head badly. I didn't tell her then how I had heard him fall that morning.

3 | Who

There is more to that story that I share later in this book. But I have to take a detour here. Without this detour, you may not understand how the stories in this book happened the way they did. But more importantly, you might not even fully understand your own stories.

As a society and as individuals, we have a deep misconception of where our thoughts, choices and actions originate. This misconception is deeply held and pervasive, so you will need to examine it for yourself to see through it. That will be much more powerful than any attempt I make to explain it directly. The exercises below will provide the opportunity to look closely at what your mind is doing. For this book to be worthwhile, keep in mind what you experience and anything you learn from these exercises.

Please take your time with this part of the book before reading later chapters. Take these questions out into your life, into your moments as they are happening, and watch very carefully for the answers. They may be very different than the answers you have while reading.

It can be hard sometimes to even notice that you're having thoughts at all. They are the all-pervasive fabric of our inner world and yet they can go completely unnoticed for much of our lives if we let them. Imagine how fish might view water. It's hard to pinpoint or grab a hold of something that is everywhere and has no observable bounds. We often don't notice the air all around us because it's usually always there. Unless it's especially cold, or blowing hard, or running out, we may not notice or think about the air around us at all. There's another complication about noticing thought. What you would in effect be noticing is the very machinery itself by which you notice and consider anything.

Your thoughts include everything. They can be about anything you're currently experiencing, including your inner emotions or anything you see, hear, taste, smell, or feel. They can be about any memory from the past, or about dreams or worries about the future. They can come up from any association at all your mind has made or be about, or in response to, other thoughts themselves. I'm asking that you generate some interest and curiosity about them, even if only until you're finished reading this book. So if you're game, let's begin.

Reading Out Loud

You'll need to get hold of another book or two. Feel free to try this once with a book you find interesting and once with one you don't, perhaps a children's book you've read too many times.

However, it has to be a book that you can read out loud and that has enough text per page so you're not constantly turning pages. *Without setting a timer*, read the book *out loud* for about two minutes. Aim for a steady but comfortable speed. You don't have to read the book loudly. But another person, if they were near enough, should be able to hear you and make out the words you are saying. Read the words steadily such that at no point is there a pause long enough to squeeze in another word or two. You'll also need a setting such that while there may be distractions, none of them should be strong enough to interrupt your reading for these couple minutes.

Please try it now before continuing.

Do you recall any thoughts that you had while reading? You at least had the thought or impulse to end the exercise or else you'd still be doing it. Eventually you had a thought of what to do next. Since you didn't set a timer, you might have had thoughts concerning if the two minutes were over yet, and how to decide that. Perhaps you had thoughts wondering: what's the point of all this, if you were doing it right, and how much that matters. You might have also had thoughts judging anything from how your voice sounded to how this exercise was designed. Then there are all the miscellaneous thoughts that could have come up about anything else at all.

So now consider those thoughts you had while reading. Were they verbal as they occurred? If so, since there weren't any long pauses in your reading, did you hear both the audio of your spoken words and the thoughts in your head at the same time? Did you just have a sense of the meaning of the thoughts, without giving words to them? If you're up for it, give it another go, maybe with a second book.

Trivial Decision

Think of some relatively trivial decision you could make, such as what to have for dinner, or what you might do this weekend. Start reading again out loud as before and make the decision. Read until you've settled on that decision or until you decide to give up, but try to give it at least a full minute. If your mind makes the decision before you even start reading, take good note of that, and try again with a different decision to make.

You may find that not only can you arrive at your trivial decision while reading, but that you can actually notice your mind bringing up and considering different options. You may even get distracted by your reading such that you forget what decision you were trying to make. But you then may find that you can *while still reading*, struggle to remember what it was, evaluate possibilities that come up, and maybe finally remember it. And *know* that you succeeded in remembering it.

Please try it now.

Making The Bed

You must be in a room that has objects you can interact with using one hand while holding an open book with the other. If you're bold enough, maybe outside at a park where there are rocks, plants and other objects you can interact with. While reading for a few minutes as we did in the previous exercise, get a sense what you can safely do at the same time. This should be done without planning exactly you'll do during these couple minutes. Feel out the limits of what you can do while the verbal part of your mind is at least partially occupied with the book you're reading.

Your eyes and mind are amazing in their ability to build up a persistent and coherent model of the world around you. They can do this even just working with your peripheral vision and momentary visual information gathered from your eyes darting around. This model is much larger than what your eyes are focused on in any given moment. You should notice not only that you can perceive quite a bit beyond the view of the book you're reading, but also that you can successfully walk around without bumping into things and manipulate objects with your free hand.

Try moving things from one part of the room to the other, turning some lights on or off, putting things into or out of the fridge or cabinets, or drawing a picture without looking at it (much). With some small effort you might even succeed in making the bed. You can decide some things ahead, but it will be valuable to see what you can come up with while reading.

Please try it now.

Immediately after writing the above, I tried this exercise while making the bed. Beforehand, I vaguely supposed I would succeed, though succeeding in whatever activities you attempt isn't the point. In the end, I was able to strip and make the bed but I was surprised that my thoughts covered a lot more ground than the logistics. Sure, there were thoughts about what to grab next and how, especially when I came to that lower fitted sheet with the elastic and I had to find a way to stretch it over the mattress with one hand while still reading the book. And of course there were thoughts about how to position the book so that my eyes could catch glimpses of what I needed next. But I found myself at the same time reacting strongly to the words I was reading from the book.

Other thoughts I didn't anticipate included: "Is this a good idea? It's probably gonna take a while." "What a waste stripping and making a bed that's already made." "OK, I see that I can do this, so do I really need to finish it?" "I want to pause for a minute and just read the book, because this part's really good." "Well now I have to finish." "I can't wait to write about this when I'm done. I'd better hurry up before I forget some of these thoughts."

Did you notice any thoughts that came up for you during the exercise? Maybe recall particular actions that you performed and consider the choices and decisions that must have been necessary in doing them. These might have included what to do and how, what's possible, and what's working. Again, try to consider the form of your thoughts and how they coexisted with the words you were reading. Were they partial words and phrases that sneaked into your brief inter-word pauses during reading? Were they in the form of images or just a sensed meaning without representation? Did you perform any actions without conscious thought of any kind?

There are many situations where we find ourselves multitasking, and if you look closely, you will notice your mind doing some very interesting things. Consider when you're speaking with someone about something complicated while walking or driving at the same time. Or when we attend to other things at the same time as we wash the dishes, eat a meal, or watch TV. Consider when you're in a conversation and without pausing, you judge the other person's reactions and change how you're speaking or what you're saying.

You can also try out variations of the exercises above whereby instead of a book, you're singing, or repeating a phrase again and again, or counting. There are many types of meditation where the verbal part of your mind is given something to keep it focused or busy. But in any of them you can easily find your mind still working on other things.

Small Action

Now consider some very small action you took recently or one you are taking while reading this. Choose one that you didn't think too hard about. It could be taking a sip of water, scratching an itch, stretching, shifting in your seat, readjusting your eyeglasses, opening the window, or turning on a lamp. Did you just start doing it, or was there some subtle urge or sensation that came up before the action? Did you choose to have the urge or thought that motivated you?

Just Watching

Spend about five minutes relatively still, just trying to notice your thoughts and any voluntary movements. When you can, notice any urge or impulse preceding a thought or action. Choose any position you can be in somewhat comfortably for the time you'll need, but not so comfortably you will fall asleep. You could be standing, laying down, sitting, eyes open or closed, whatever you find works best. Feel free to try a few different things before settling in. But note that this exercise does not in any way depend on you being perfectly comfortable or relaxed. You may try it more than once using different poses, for example, sitting with eyes open or standing with eyes closed. Don't set a timer; the exact amount of time is not important. But don't fall too short of five minutes. Feel free to have a timepiece nearby that you can glance at if and when you wish. But if you do, see if you can get a close look at any thoughts or actions around that. If and when you get lost in thought, try to continue this exercise with the very next thought.

Please try it now.

Life Of A Thought

The next exercise is similar, but this time try to catch specifically *how* thoughts arise in your mind. This may include any feelings, sensations or urges right before and as the thought forms, as well as the forms the thought takes. Does it come in one word at a time? Or is there a sense of meaning first that provokes words, pictures, and other symbols? Do different thoughts come in differently? If it comes in as a fully formed sentence, can you cut off the sentence and still *know* the meaning intended? If it comes in as images, how sharp are they, do details come in over time? Does the meaning evolve as you think the thought?

It's valuable to stick with this exercise even if you are having difficulties. Your mind may try different ways to succeed. The kinds of thoughts you have and how they come in may change. All the while, you're becoming more experienced. See if you can get closer and closer to the birth of your thoughts. Push the edge of your awareness as far as you can. What is the earliest point in the process of thoughts and impulses arising that you can be aware of?

Please try it now.

Hopefully you stayed with these last two exercises even if you found them frustrating, overwhelming, or unfair. Your sustained effort here was valuable regardless of how well things seemed to go. Rather than being about actually achieving a certain goal or mental state, your effort in attempting to do so sets the stage to closely observe how your mind works. If you cut these exercises short or have any other reason you might want to give them one more go, please do so before reading on.

Now consider your experiences of watching thoughts and impulses as they arose in your consciousness. Reflect on whatever you were able to catch as earliest moments of a thought appearing or coming together. Drawing upon these experiences, let's push the line of questioning I introduced this book with a little further.

- Do you choose to have the thoughts that you do?
- When various urges or impulses come up, do you choose for them to come up?
- When you make choices, do you choose to prefer what you do?

Or is it that at some point, at some level, as far as you can consciously experience and control, you just have the thought?

Whether your thoughts arise from the current state of the universe, God, quantum randomness, your unconscious, the balance of chemicals in your brain, or any combination of things, *you* don't choose the thoughts and emotional reactions that you have. To consciously choose them would involve more thoughts, and how would those be chosen? To say that your thoughts come from your soul doesn't change the situation. You're still not consciously choosing your thoughts or the soul that gives them to you. At times you may have thoughts that are in line with your goals; at others thoughts that you wish you didn't have. But in either case you didn't choose for them to appear. They came without your asking for them.

What about when you proactively choose your environment, the people you associate with, the activities and media you engage with, the habits you work to build or abandon, everything under your control to influence how you will make future choices and decisions? Those involve decisions to put those things in place. And you didn't choose to have the thoughts that helped you make those decisions. Of course those are still incredibly helpful life choices to make and I hope we make them well.

For example, you decide to not bring any more junk food into your home, so that when you want a snack you eat something healthier. That may turn out to be a great decision that works wonderfully. But you didn't choose to decide that. The thought to do so came to you or was given to you, and it resonated with you enough to stick. Thoughts and feelings to the contrary: that such a plan won't work, or that you'll just overeat later when you go out, or that you can control yourself even with the junk food around, didn't come to you or weren't persuasive enough.

But you didn't choose or decide those things. We can feel what hooks or resonates with us. We can tell which option feels the most "right", but we don't choose for it to feel that way. If healthy choices resonate most with you, then that's the mental landscape that you're working with right now. See it as divine grace or great fortune.

There are times when instead unhelpful thoughts come in stronger, when we resonate more with the feelings that drive us to worse choices; times when the thoughts that would lead us away from a poor decision either don't come, or don't hook us. Consider the bad habits, the moments of procrastination, the character flaws, all the problems we get hung up on. Did we choose them? Do we choose to have the thoughts that support them?

If we don't have conscious control over our thoughts, how much control do we have over the actions motivated and sustained by those thoughts? I'm not saying choices and decisions aren't being made. They certainly are and some are pretty poor or even horrifying. I'm not saying people aren't or shouldn't be hurt or angered by the outcome of those horrible choices, decisions, and actions. I've been plenty hurt by some of them, and I've been overwhelmingly angry. And very sad. Terrible things have happened and do happen.

When things go wrong, where does responsibility lie and what amount of punishment is deserved?

I'm not saying that there isn't anything to be done. But to even know what needs be done, we have to look deeply at what our inner experience of living as a human being actually is. This knowledge changes what makes sense to be done when things go wrong. What would be most helpful to the current situation? How can we encourage better future choices? How can we effectively, ethically, and compassionately deter future poor choices?

What does it mean to say choices and decisions are being made, but not by *you*? There you are: living your life, making decisions, doing as you decided, and experiencing the consequences. But there is no independent *consciousness* or *you* separate from everything else. Your each and every thought and action only makes sense, and in fact can only exist, in the context of *everything else*.

In thinking about all this, you may start to feel as if you're just being blown about by the wind. But remember that you are simultaneously influencing all the things that are influencing you. More than simple cause and effect, it's a system where everything is interdependent on everything else. You're certainly not just a leaf in the wind. If anything, you are also the wind and all the other leaves. But even given that, here *you* are.

4 | Punishment

When anyone, including ourselves, does the wrong thing, we feel that they could have and should have done the right thing instead. There's something that they should have remembered or realized sooner, or noticed more, or known more about. They should have known better or been more careful. What they were doing should have felt too wrong to continue. But in spite of how strongly we feel that things should have gone differently, whatever happened *is what happened*. Whether or not we understand the causes, that person thought what they thought and therefore they did what they did.

As we've explored, whether someone appears to do something right or wrong, they didn't choose to have the thoughts that they did. Still, we usually blame people for their failings, and then punish them. We may beat ourselves up over our own mistakes, asking how could we have been so stupid or clumsy. When others fall short, we may judge or treat them poorly. We may retaliate with words and actions against those we feel have wronged us. Even the negative feelings we harbor towards them can affect how we treat them and how we speak to others about them.

In the stories that follow, I want to look into our concept of blame and into the effects of our punishments.

Wedding Band

One day, I was laying down in a grassy field in Prospect Park, enjoying the warm sun and a blue sky. I got up to go home and, after walking for a few minutes, I realized I wasn't wearing my wedding band. I'd lost it, again. I figured that it must have fallen off in the field, and turned around. Trying hard to remember, I vaguely had a sense of where I was laying in the field. I was looking through the grass for it, trying to notice anything shiny, metallic. Instead of my ring I'm was finding bits of shiny gum wrappers, coins, and soda can tabs.

But did I even lose it here? I tried to remember if I had it when I lay down. But why would I remember either way? I had purposely chosen a comfortable ring that I wouldn't notice all the time. Turns out that my efforts led to too loose of a ring.

After looking for while, I was ready to call it quits. Though it was a nice looking wedding band, it was made of titanium and cost only $12 online. I didn't need that one back, especially since it wasn't the original anyway. I had lost that one the month before.

But just as I was getting up to leave, somebody saw me looking in the grass and asked me what I was looking for. When I told him, he became determined to help. He called his friend over so they could both help me find my ring. I told them not to worry; that it was lost at this point as I had already looked pretty hard for it; that I would just replace it. But they would hear none of it. I couldn't bring myself to explain that it was just a cheap ring that didn't have much sentimental value to me. *My marriage* is priceless to me; *the ring* was not.

So we all looked together for something that didn't need to be found.

I would have much rather just spent another $12 at that point. Eventually, I decided that I didn't want anyone spending any more time on this, so I told them it was OK and I was heading home. They asked for my phone number so they could call me when they found the ring. I wouldn't give it to them, because I wanted them to give up like I had. But after all their effort, I was then too ashamed to tell them it was all for nothing. I awkwardly walked away.

I was upset that I had lost another ring and I wasn't looking forward to my wife finding out. But I was even more upset with myself for how I handled the whole situation, having wasted other people's time and acted so odd just because I couldn't say what needed to be said. Turns out the third time was a charm. The next ring I bought was a half size smaller, and five years later I still haven't lost it. A backup ring that I bought at the same time collects dust.

-=-=-=-=-=-

Through one lens, many things in this story could have gone differently. I could have:

- Done better research to buy the right size ring the first time.
- Decided the ring felt loose and exchanged it.
- Noticed the ring falling off as it happened.
- Not turned around to look for the ring at all.
- Confessed that the ring was cheap, and not the original at any rate.

Yet through another lens, whether or not we understand why, things unfolded *exactly* the way that they should have and therefore *did*. I'm not referring here to what we would personally view as ideal, what would accord with our expectations, or what could be seen as even acceptable in general. I'm referring to the way that things had to proceed given the full situation. I believe that nothing is helped by insisting that the past should have gone otherwise. We influence, but don't have control over:

- what grabs our attention
- how long it takes for something to dawn on us
- what options occur to us

Still, we *must* do our best. Sometimes our "best" will not be our best; it may even be a disaster. But we must still always give our best effort if we want the best possible outcome. We need to focus on improving the present and planning a better future.

I believe that, too often, we waste our emotional energy on blame and cause a lot of unnecessary suffering with our punishments. My hope is for us to shift our energy to understanding and helping.

Final Assignment

I used to work as an electrical engineer for a managed long term care (MLTC) company in New York City. MLTC companies coordinate care and services for individuals with disabilities and chronic illnesses. For many, that company was indispensable, providing services that no other organization would. Working there, I built equipment for individuals with significant paralysis, which empowered them to control their TV, lights, hospital bed, windows, and air conditioner, among other things. The devices I built restored a significant amount of independence to these individuals, often bringing a smile to their face while lessening the tremendous workload of their caregivers.

Since most of my clients had unique situations, I often had to build these devices in their home to get things just right. I usually had to bring a significant amount of tools and parts to their home from my workshop. Unexpected situations requiring special tools and parts came up regularly. I learned to significantly overpack to cover as many contingencies as possible.

After several years, that company finally closed their doors due to long-term funding issues. While this was hard for me and the rest of the staff, it was especially painful for those individuals who needed our help. I had my work cut out for me near the end. Many clients reached out to me with requests, knowing that this was their last chance to get my help.

My last house call of the last day was up in the Bronx, several hours away from my workshop. Partway into my work at the client's home, I realized I couldn't finish the job; I had forgotten to pack something. I was devastated. "How could I forget to bring that! Why today?" With no store nearby to get what I needed, I had to just apologize and pack everything back up.

-=-=-=-=-=-

We may take remembering things for granted, but do we even know how or why we remember? Unless we've set up something explicitly to remind us, we're relying on our mind to do the "right" thing. And either our mind bubbles up the right thought at the right time or it doesn't. There are techniques to improve our memory, but we still don't control which things we remember and which slip our mind. I believe we should not be hard on someone just because their mind didn't remind them of something. We need to stop acting as if people have control over things which they do not.

Of course, we can set some reminder. But we would need to decide to do that. Instead we may think to ourselves, "I've done this dozens of times now, I'll be fine." or "I'm sure I won't forget. There's no way I wouldn't realize it if I forgot it." Again, we have to work with the fact that we do not choose our thoughts. So let's proactively set ourselves up for success whenever we can, but still show ourselves some compassion when we fall short.

Pickpocket

When I was thirty, I spent a week in Trinidad with a friend who lived there. Toward the end of my visit, Carnival was taking place. The festival of Carnival in Trinidad is so big, so colorful, so incredibly energetic. Huge crowds and a contagious positive energy are everywhere. I tagged along with my friend and his brothers to J'ouvert. I rarely dance but I was pulled right in along with everyone else. Someone dancing near me smiled and covered me in colorful powder, and I followed the huge Music Trucks through the streets. I was having an amazing time.

At some point, I briefly felt someone's hand in my back pocket. Then again. This didn't alarm me too much since I didn't have anything in there. But after the third or fourth time I thought "come on already" and turned around. Seeing the kid who was trying so hard, I gave him a look that implied, "Really?" He shrugged his shoulders and gave me a look that seemed to reply, "Well, yeah."

I was wearing my usual beat up clothes, but I still looked like a tourist and probably had some money. I'm sure I looked like an easy mark. Neither of us said anything and I turned back around and continued dancing alongside the Music Trucks. I wasn't mad at him. I'll note here that I didn't choose my emotional response; it's what came up. Looking back, I'm happy I was able to just brush it off.

Bent Glasses

Five years earlier, I was walking home late one night. Even with my iPod's headphones in my ear, I thought I heard steps behind me. Finally, at the next corner, I turned around to face whoever it was, but he turned down the other street.

I continued walking. I had just mentally moved on when someone ahead walked right up to me while the other guy came back around from behind. They pinned me against a large white van parked there. They ripped the iPod from my hand and knocked my glasses off. With a hand tight around my throat, one of them asked me for my wallet several times. All I kept saying through my restricted airway was "I got no money." They eventually gave up and ran off. I still have no idea why I didn't just give them my wallet nor why they didn't just take it out of my pocket. It took me a minute to find my twisted glasses on the ground. I slowly bent them back while trying not to snap them. They didn't feel quite right. Neither did my throat. I walked over to some people standing outside their apartment building just two doors down. I asked them "Did you see that?" The reply I received was "Sorry, I didn't see anything."

I felt hurt and angry. I was much more upset at those people standing outside than the two people who attacked me. "Why wouldn't they help me?! I *know* they saw the whole thing." In hindsight, I can easily imagine many reasons why they would want to stay out of it. But in that moment, I actually felt more understanding towards the two robbers than my supposed witnesses. Again, I didn't choose any of these emotional responses. I felt what I felt.

Tow Truck

In high school, as the first among my friends to have a driver's license, I frequently drove my friends around in the $300 car I fixed up. One day, a friend wanted to visit an auto salvage yard, the type where you pick-and-pull the parts yourself from the car, and pay for them as you leave. Four of us went together and my friend found the carburetor he was looking for. He removed it from the car, and put it in his backpack. Some time later, when we were at the far back edge of the property, my friend took the carburetor out of his backpack and threw it over the barbed wire fence out of the salvage yard. Looking back, I can't believe I didn't register what I was getting involved in.

We took the scenic route to the front gate. They checked our bags; and we left. I drove us down to where my friend asked me to stop so he could hop out. He walked along the fence to where the carburetor had landed, picked it up and was walking back when I noticed a large tow truck in my rear-view mirror. It was coming our way fast.

We yelled to my friend to hurry up. I was terrified of the tow truck but I also didn't want to abandon my friend. Somehow I decided to just slowly drive the car forward. My friend ran as fast as he could and jumped into the car. I floored it, but it was an old Dodge Colt and, moments later, the tow truck easily caught up to us, pulled ahead, and turned across the road, blocking us. Somebody in my car yelled for me to backup, but I gave up and turned my engine off.

Three guys jumped out of the tow truck and walked over. One of them opened the rear passenger-side door where my friend had jumped in and pulled him out.

I heard them slam his head against my car.

Another told the rest of us to get out of the car. We did. The police arrived and asked if the salvage yard wanted to press charges, but they just wanted to file a formal complaint. I found out later that this was the only way they could get better patrolling of the area by local police.

-=-=-=-=-=-

Consider some of the choices made by the high school students and the salvage yard staff. Imagine the thoughts and impulses that came up for them at various points. Try to imagine which options didn't occur to them. Recall what you know experientially about how thoughts and impulses arise in your own mind.

The characters of that story *did* make many choices. But they did not choose the things that formed those choices including their thoughts, impulses, which things they noticed, and which options occurred to them.

Following this line of thought begs the question: is nobody ever guilty? Can someone just do whatever they want and remain innocent? On one hand it feels like that *can't* possibly be right. The person who committed the crime or made the mistake *has* to be held accountable, right? Isn't that the main way we deter crime and mistakes in the first place? It can't be that we are just using each person as the scapegoat for their own actions. Are we? After all, they are the person who performed that action. But if, as we've explored together, you don't choose your own thoughts and impulses, to what degree are you accountable for the actions they fuel?

When we make a mistake or someone else wrongs us, we can address it the way we always have. But does it achieve what is really needed? Consider the times you've given other people a piece of your mind. Consider the times you've been hard on yourself. How often did it really change you for the better or improve the situation?

When we punish ourselves and others, what is the total outcome? The target of our punishment may "do better" next time, but how do they feel about themselves? How do they feel about us? And as the one delivering the punishment, how do we feel about ourselves? Are we being who we want to be? Are we finding the peace of mind we're looking for?

Consider what is achieved by the negative emotions produced, especially over time. The recipient may be motivated to avoid repeating their mistake. But if to them, things seem unfair, outside their control, or too hard to face, they may instead be motivated to get better at hiding or justifying their mistakes. Instead of wanting to understand and improve the situation, we could all wind up just wanting to escape it. Should we accept all that as the cost of "getting it off our chest"? Is it all worth it to make sure that they know how "wrong" they were?

In this book, I'm focusing on how we as individuals punish ourselves and others. As a society, of course there are clear reasons to deal with criminals directly and swiftly including to limit further damage they may cause. However, it is crucial that we do not stop there. We must look further. Ignoring the cultural and environmental influences that contributed to their behavior is just asking for more of the same or worse.

Further, when we act as if a person can control every aspect of their mind or the universe of outside influence, I believe *we* are committing a crime. This crime does not only hurt that person. There is a deep effect on everyone who is witness to it playing out.

The Bus

Once a friend of mine hopped on a New York City SBS bus. For SBS buses, you're supposed pay ahead of time at machines near the bus stops. You get a receipt, which occasionally you'll be asked to show as proof you paid.

My friend was rushing and didn't want to miss the bus, so he hopped on without paying. He didn't want to get caught later without a receipt, so at the next stop he asked the bus driver to hold the bus while he hopped out to quickly pay at a machine. He planned to hop back on the bus after he got a receipt. But when he got off, the bus pulled off.

My friend quickly went from shock to anger. He had asked the driver to hold the bus and had received no indication that the driver couldn't or wouldn't wait for him. So my friend quickly decided, "No. Not this time! He's *not* gonna get away with this!" Backpack and all he sprinted across busy streets after the bus, and caught it at the next stop. He went in through the open door toward the back and, with his adrenaline going, he pushed through the crowded bus and started yelling at the driver.

It's worth noting that the bus driver was still driving the bus during this. The safety of everyone on that bus including my friend depended on the bus driver keeping his focus on the road. But for my friend in that moment, the only thing that mattered was that the bus driver *knew* the full extent of what he had done wrong.

-=-=-=-=-=-

Maybe at times we've completely given up on improving things. Maybe all we care about is feeling better and so we just let them have it. But do we feel better in the long run? Is there another way?

5 | Calm

A Hug

It was a Sunday morning, pretty early. I went out just for a walk. I had some time and intended on really being present for it. Feeling each step on the ground, hearing the sounds of passing cars, sounds of birds, seeing the clouds in the sky, the beauty and uniqueness of each tree, feeling the breeze. I wanted to be there for all of it.

Across from the grocery store, I watched a woman parking a car beside some traffic cones on the street. Something felt odd about her parking there, even temporarily. She had also parked right up against the cones, almost running them over. The car stayed still for a bit, but as I got closer I noticed the woman cut her wheels hard to her left. The act of steering the wheels pushed the cones. I heard the road sound of another car approaching quickly. I heard her engine rev up as the woman stepped hard on the gas. I barely had time to register the sense of doom.

You could hear the skidding tires as a truck smashed into her car and pushed it several feet. There was a silence. The woman got out of her car, visibly shaking and sobbing, but she was standing.

Then the driver of the truck got out, and he started yelling at her. She just continued sobbing, her hand over her mouth, as he continued yelling. She certainly must not have looked before darting her car into the oncoming traffic. But however clear her blame seemed, it was equally clear that she was devastated. It was mid-sentence that he stopped yelling at her. He took three steps forward to close the distance between them, put his arms around her, and hugged her as she sobbed on his shoulder. After she had calmed down and was no longer sobbing he walked back towards his truck. He opened the rear passenger seat door to check on the old lady sitting there.

-=-=-=-=-=-

There are ways to notice when we are punishing ourselves and others, and to stop. But even when we have every intention to be more aware and to pause more often, it's likely that many times we won't see what we're doing. It's also likely that sometimes we will see it, but we won't want to stop. We won't want to think about what's happening. When our emotions are too strong and what we might see would be too painful to look at. But these moments are often the ones with the most going wrong and with the most desperate need for our full attention and care.

To pause and then be willing to significantly change course requires strong motivation. It must be especially powerful if it is to win out no matter what we are in the midst of saying or doing. One place we can find this motivation is in the compassion and love we have for ourselves and others. When it is strong enough, and if we open our eyes, we'll feel incredibly moved to stop what we're doing.

To get us there, we may need to build more compassion than we've had in the past. I believe we can find more compassion for ourselves by developing and applying our understanding of our mind's workings. We should continue to observe how our thoughts arise and how our decisions are made, especially when things go wrong. As we achieve this even sporadically, we'll gain a deeper sense of what we're working with and the larger base from which all this arises. Over time what we discover will naturally fuel more self-compassion. Once we have a strong sense of compassion for ourselves we can apply our understanding to others, fueling our compassion for them.

There may be people who we want to see as utterly other than ourselves. It's hard for us to feel compassion for them. We may be angered or repulsed by their past or current life choices. We feel strongly that we do not have have any connection or similarity to those people. But such a standpoint can be incredibly dangerous. It lends itself too easily to ignoring, or even causing, the suffering of others. And if we look closely, such a standpoint also doesn't square with how things actually work.

No matter how different our circumstances seem, we are all connected in countless ways. Our futures are bound to each other and to this planet. Each of our joys and sufferings have ripple effects far beyond our own lives. We can see this on a global scale through wars and other large scale acts of violence as tensions boil over. It's seen when trash dumped off the coast of one country washes up on the shore of another. It's also apparent in how a portion of the world's population can increase global warming causing devastating climate change and storms for others across the planet. On the individual level, we can see how our suffering affects others when we take out our anger on someone who has nothing to do with what is really bothering us. If the recipient doesn't have the ability to understand and transform what we've dumped on them, they may soon be dumping it on someone else.

Further, regardless of all the ways we are unique from each other, the core of our human situation is the same. We are all working with our past, desires, thoughts, and human needs & weaknesses whether we want them or not. No matter how at odds we think we are at each other, we share so many aspects of both our inner and outer worlds. On top of all this, if we look closely enough at how each of us is affecting and is affected by everyone else, then in a way there is no real separation between any of us. Unfortunately, we either never realize this or easily forget it. This often happens even with those we are closest to.

Hold It

Probably almost ten years ago, I was out with a friend for a walk. She was going to check in her bag and wanted to first hand me the tall travel mug she was holding. She extended it to me, her hand wrapped around the middle of it. I grabbed it one-handed from underneath. A moment after she let go, she said with a faint agitation, "Would you hold it?" I replied "I am holding it." She protested a little more forcefully, "No, would you *hold* it please?" I replied with a little more assertiveness, "I *am* holding it." This escalated a bit as it went back and forth. At some point, I think I even shook my hand with the mug and said, "See, it's fine! I got it!" Finally, completely exasperated, she exclaimed, "Are you testing me?"

-=-=-=-=-=-

I knew from the very first sign of her agitation exactly how she wanted me to hold her mug. I also knew that her request came from her worry that something would go wrong. Maybe I would spill it, maybe the top would come off, maybe it would slip out of my grasp if I got bumped by someone or tripped. It just didn't look secure to her. But I didn't want to be told what to do or how something so simple ought to be done. And I disagreed with her assessment of the situation. So I was going to *prove* that I was right. Maybe I thought to myself, "If she's getting upset about this, then that's on her."

If I had paused for a moment and looked, I might have considered that it was her mug after all. Shouldn't she get to decide how it's handled? Also, if my actions are upsetting her, and I'm trying to provoke a reaction, that's on me actually. If I'm deeply upsetting a close friend and myself, is this really worth it? Is this even the best way make my point?

Which brings us most importantly to: what was I really achieving? What could I have even imagined achieving, especially as it was escalating? There's almost no imaginable scenario whereby she would suddenly say to me, "You're right, I was being silly." How could I expect her not to get increasingly upset as I ignored her requests? How could I expect brash actions to address her worries? But I didn't pause to see any of that. If I had, perhaps *I* could have said, "You're right."

Many times, when emotions are escalating we would be well-advised to pause and seriously consider our actions. We have to ask ourselves, "Is this what I want to be doing?" "Is this who I want to be?" "Is this working?" If it's not, we need to stop what we're doing, *right now*. And then if something actually still needs doing, we can look for a better way.

If we want to take good care of ourselves and others, if we don't want to keep making things worse, then we need to observe closely what is happening. This includes everything going on inside of us and everything that we are adding to the total situation. More often than our anger being a call to action, it's a call to stop and look. Almost no matter what we're in the middle of saying or doing we can always pause and open our eyes.

Only when we see and accept things as they really are in this moment do we stand a fair chance of making things better rather than worse. And when we catch a glimpse, whether intentionally or by accident, we must not ignore what we see. Sometimes, to our complete dismay, we'll discover that our previous view was incomplete or even deeply mistaken. In these moments we *can* turn on a dime. It may seem awkward to turn about-face so suddenly but we don't choose when something dawns on us. However, we can choose to change course when we glimpse the devastating outcome we're heading towards. We need not identify with our current action and be bound to it, we can be more.

The anger, hurt, and other strong emotions of other people are also a call to stop and look. We often meet their anger or hurt with our own anger or defensiveness. "Why are they attacking me?" "Why am I to blame for their situation or their emotions?" "I can't be held responsible for that!" "That's not my problem." "They brought this upon themselves." But instead of giving in to our habitual ways of shielding ourselves from discomfort or accountability, we need to listen carefully to what the situation is telling us. Our actions may or may not be hurting someone. But we'll never find out if all we care about is making sure we're not seen as "wrong." Instead we need to focus on what is actually going wrong and how we might help. Otherwise it is too easy for us to bring suffering to ourselves and others without even realizing it.

Medicine

Sometimes we decide that even if this gets ugly then that's just the way it's going to have to be. We get locked into our course of action. The more suffering our plan causes and accrues, the more we can't abandon it, for that would mean we caused all that pain for no reason.

And that we were wrong, very wrong.

One time my daughter, then two years old, was pretty sick with an ear infection. Her pediatrician prescribed a particular antibiotic and for whatever reason she absolutely refused to drink it. It was the first dose, which is often the hardest because she wasn't into any rhythm with it yet. But I was also particularly eager to get her started on it since she really wasn't feeling well.

All the old tricks didn't work. Whatever I mixed it in, she still tasted it and spit it out. When I tried distracting her with a movie, she still refused to open her mouth. Bribing didn't work. Explaining it to her and towing a hard line didn't work. I called her pediatrician for advice, but she had nothing.

My daughter was sick and it was my duty to get her to take her medicine. Failure wasn't an option. But nothing I tried was working.

So I exercised the nuclear option: With one of my arms, I held her to me and forced her arms down, while with my other arm I used an oral syringe to squirt the medicine into her mouth. She hated it and was squirming. I hated it too, but I could do it. In the past I had felt I had no choice but to pin her down for shots at the doctor, strep tests where they rub the back of your throat with a cotton swab, some really upset diaper changes, and wrestling her into her stroller when she absolutely didn't want to go. This type of thing was always a last resort but I would do it if necessary. It seemed necessary again now. Restraining her in this way, I squeezed a small bit in at a time because I didn't want her to choke on it. She gagged a little on the first bit but swallowed it. I felt horrible, but it did work. However, she vomited up everything on the second bit. I was very wrong. This was *not* the way.

At some point later we found the magic formula: Mixing the medicine with juice and lots of honey, in her favorite yellow cup, and with a straw. We gave it to her while she watched a fun video as she sat on my lap. I'd start the video and let her know I would pause it soon if she didn't take a sip. After a sip I'd let the video go a bit and if she didn't take another sip, I'd remind her that I'd have to pause the video. In the end, after a few pauses, she wanted the video to go straight through, so she drank the all her medicine quickly.

That formula didn't work forever, but with some luck and creativity we could always figure something out. My desperation had been real. The imperative to solve the problem was real. But the deep feeling of wrongness I felt in forcing the medicine on my daughter was also real. We don't always have the answer. But if we pause and accept that fact, and the emotions that come with it, we have a better shot of finding a real answer. The best intentions and the best efforts can still cause real suffering, especially if we are not open to seeing all that is available for us to see, moment to moment.

Mario Bros.

One day, my elementary school sent a note home that they were recommending speech therapy. It was free and would be provided at school. Among other issues, I had a lot of trouble pronouncing L's and R's correctly. My dad decided that their assessment was ridiculous and that he could fix my problems right on the spot. He called me into his room and he gave me some words to say out loud. I tried, but they came out incorrectly. He barked at me to try again, yet I kept failing. He yelled at me that I wasn't trying, and commanded me to say them right this time. I still couldn't do it. He yelled at me asking if I was trying to make him angry. I was sobbing at this point. He began threatening his belt.

Literally for the life of me, I couldn't say the words right. At some point, he gave up and told me to get out of his sight. I remember, days later at school, enjoying the speech classes. Especially the ten minutes of playing Mario Bros. that we ended each class with.

-=-=-=-=-=-

We must be willing to adjust or even abandon our views whenever they conflict with what is in front of us. In this story, my dad was sure that I could overcome my speech problems, on the spot. If he had paused, and looked, he would have seen a child trying incredibly hard and still unable to succeed. My dad also accused me of trying to provoke his anger. But if he opened his eyes, he would have seen a trembling child, giving his all to *escape* his father's anger. There wasn't defiance in my eyes, rather there was a growing terror. My dad's plan may have been to scare me into pronouncing things correctly. But it was plain to see that my increased sobbing and stuttering was instead leading to *worse* pronunciation.

If we want to avoid heaping unnecessary suffering on ourselves and others, we need to keep our eyes open. We have to take notice of the uncomfortable emotions of those around us. We can't continue to put off addressing what we see. It's also important to catch, and respond appropriately, when someone is "locked in" to their current plan, unable to see any alternative, or when someone is running on autopilot. It can be invaluable to ask: What is each of us trying to do in this situation, and is it working?

Picking up on these types of cues can remind us to pause. But once reminded, please, do actually pause, and look. Doing so while keeping in mind what we all actually have control over can generate the compassion we need to stop punishing ourselves and others.

Everyone we're dealing with, including ourselves, is human. There's always going to be times when we get angry. And, of course, our actions will sometimes get someone else angry. We're still going to do things we regret. And we're still going to have all sorts of problems to accept and work on. What we're talking about here doesn't remove or explain away any part of ourselves or our lives. That's all still there including all the problems. What changes is how we can view those things. And that changes everything.

By viewing things differently, hopefully we won't create as many additional problems. The people we struggle with need not be seen as if they're out to get us, or their actions as a personal attack against us. We don't have to feel at war with our coworkers, our family, our friends, or the strangers we interact with. We may see how the other person *isn't* trying to "push our buttons" or "test us". All of this, in turn, changes how we choose what to do next. At times, we punish ourselves as if we had wanted to make a mess of things all along. I hope we finally stop.

None of this is a suggestion to deny your feelings, or dismiss them as irrational. That's both dangerous and unhelpful. Those feelings are the feelings you have, and you need to acknowledge them. They provide crucial information about what is currently happening inside and out. They also often provide cues to pause and sometimes to change course. If we don't look into and process our feelings, we are ignoring what they are telling us. When eventually the circumstances behind them become more dire, we will be forced to acknowledge them and, by then, we will be in a much worse situation. What I am suggesting is that we do not reflexively strike out in response to our painful feelings.

There are actions we can take to make it more likely that we'll pause when we need to. When the thought to pause does pop up we should *actually listen to it and pause*. This isn't just to benefit that instance. If we do not action this thought, its frequency will decline over time and it fade into the background as it becomes irrelevant. But when we do action it, more connections form to it in our mind. It can become a more and more ingrained habit. For it to become second nature we must allow ourselves to pause especially when other thoughts push us not to.

We should proactively exercise our awareness of our emotional states and thoughts as they arise. This awareness will help us notice when to pause and when we're not being who we want to be. When we do pause, this awareness will help us see what is actually going on. There are many activities we can do regularly and many we can try throughout the day to build our awareness. These activities can also help steady us so that we act in accordance with our true values. They also can be a source of peace and happiness that nourishes us.

6 | Flow

Can we resolve not to punish anymore? To do so, we would have to find ways to flow and work with what is. We would aim to accept circumstances and people as they are in this moment, because they are already here as they are. This doesn't mean that they can't or won't change, or that we can't effect any change. And this doesn't mean that we have to allow problems to continue. Sometimes swift or forceful action *is* warranted. But we need to start from where we are, and avoid punishing out of denial, anger or shame. Then we can shift our energy to accepting, understanding, and helping.

On The Side
One night, a friend and I were walking outside, looking for a place to grab dinner. He eventually recalled a Mexican restaurant he really liked. The weather was good and we planned to take it to-go so we could eat outside in a nearby park. We stepped inside, looked at the menu, and both settled on burritos. I ordered mine first and asked for it with guacamole. The cashier said sure, but that it would be "on the side" unless I ordered it as "super" which was $3 more. Then the guacamole,

salsa, and sour cream would be inside the burrito, and I would get the chunkier salsa. I didn't want to spend the $3 so I said on the side was fine. Then my friend ordered his burrito, asked for sour cream, and then wanted to make sure it was on the inside of the burrito. The cashier gave him the same option she gave me of "super" for $3 more.

My friend said, "But why would you ever put it outside? I mean, it's a burrito, it's useless outside. What do people even do with that? There's nothing you can do with that." The cashier responded, "I'm sorry. Well, sometimes people dip it." My friend came back with "Really?" Then the cashier said "OK, I'll go ask to see what they can do for you." and she left to ask her manager. My friend turned to me and said, "I guess I was sorta being a jerk." The cashier came back a minute later and told my friend that his sour cream will be on the inside. Then she asked me if I wanted my guacamole on the inside as well.

A Muffin

I was at one of my favorite bagel shops. The way it's organized there, you have to place your order with one of the cooks. They make it and bring it to the cashier, telling them what your ordered. At that point, with your food ready and the cashier knowing what you ordered, you can pay. The two people ahead of me in line had each placed their orders with cooks who were now busy cooking. That day, I just wanted a muffin and I saw a good-looking one on display in arm's reach of the cashier. She was looking at her cell phone, I guessed just killing time. So I went directly to her and asked for the muffin. She said I had to place the order with a cook. I replied, "But they're busy with someone else's order. I just want that muffin right there, that's all." She gave me a dirty look and said, "You just don't get it, do you? Do you need me to place your order for you?" I was fuming inside. It wasn't that I didn't know how to place the order; it's that I thought this whole system was dumb and didn't make any sense. I walked back over to the cooks and, when they were ready, I placed my order for the muffin. The cook walked over to the display case, grabbed the muffin, put it in a bag, and handed it to the cashier. I paid and left without saying anything. But in my head, I was thinking, "What was the big deal?! Was it that hard to put a muffin in a bag?"

In hindsight I suppose she could have also been thinking, "What's the big deal? Why can't you wait a few minutes for it to be your turn?" For all I know, she was instructed that all orders have to come through the cooks first. But I didn't pause to wonder about anything like that. To me, at that moment, whatever her reasoning was, whatever the rules were, my way of looking at it made perfect sense, so I was right. Any procedure to the contrary was stupid, and anyone following it was just being stubborn or worse. But did I really need a special exception made for me? I didn't try to understand why things were as they were. There wasn't any rush on my end, but I felt wronged on principle. I felt I shouldn't have to wait if there was someone who could help me and, as I saw it, had nothing else to do. I was so angry that she implied I couldn't follow a simple instruction.

But the truth was I couldn't.

Couple Pages Left

When I was twenty-three, I lived in New Jersey and rode the train to work each day. I don't remember what prompted it, but I wanted to reread *The Little Prince* by Antoine de Saint-Exupéry, a book I loved from my childhood. So one morning, I packed it into my backpack to read during the train ride home after work. I only had ten or so pages left as the train rolled into my station. I threw the book into by backpack, zipped it up, and hopped off the train.

It was late and very dark, but the weather was warm and there wasn't a cloud in the sky. During my walk home, I came to the small bridge, one end of which had a street lamp overhead. The thought came to me that this would be a great place to finish the book. Standing on the bridge's walkway, I took off my backpack and reached into it to pull out my book. Around this time, a car passed over the bridge, one of the few cars I saw since getting off the train. I pulled out the book, sat down, and in the almost perfect silence I resumed reading.

Minutes later, a police car pulled up with lights flashing. As he got out of the car, two other police cars pulled up with their lights flashing. The first police officer asked me what I was doing; I replied that I was reading a book. He told me that they received a call about suspicious activity on the bridge, and he strongly suggested that I go home to read my book. I was pretty upset, and felt that I was "in the right". I hadn't broken any laws. So I told the officer I was almost done and wanted to finish it right where I was. The other officers were out of their cars at this point. They discussed briefly then the first one told me I could finish my book but that they would wait right there until I left. So I read the rest of *The Little Prince* a few feet from three police officers and their cars, all lightbars still flashing. After I finished, I packed the book into my backpack, and continued my walk.

I don't remember any other words being exchanged. But I do remember after not too many steps, the flashing from the lightbars ceasing and hearing the police cars pull away. On many levels, my actions there seem pretty foolish to me now. Why did I need to give them a hard time? Was this really a "right under attack" that I had to defend? If they did receive a call about suspicious activity, then they were just doing their job.

Turn Signal

I have a lot of respect for NYC taxi and ride-sharing drivers. For me, it would be a really stressful job. To do it well, you have to push the limits of your driving ability and depend on other drivers to do the right thing more than you can guarantee. Also, the ride can take longer than it "should" due to traffic and other factors outside your control. Then you get worse tips, worse reviews, and miss out on other rides you could be being paid for. During one ride I took home, someone changed lanes without signaling right in front of my driver as he was accelerating. He avoided the accident, but he *needed* the other driver to learn a lesson.

He took the next exit to follow them, even though that was slightly out of our way. He pulled our car alongside the left of hers at the stop at the end of the off-ramp. He then opened his passenger window, and motioned for her to open her window. When she did, he asked her "So do you even have a driver's license?!" She replied "What?!" He went on to explain, "When you change lanes, you gotta signal. That's what you have signals for. Learn to drive!" Then he drove off. Later, during that same ride, another driver again failed to signal. He just leaned on his horn and vented out loud to himself. He didn't avoid encountering more "bad drivers." And based on how offended the first one seemed, I don't think she was going to learn any lessons or take any advice from him.

Double-Parked

A common scene of frustration in my neighborhood is someone double parking temporarily on a narrow one-way street. There's barely enough room for other cars to get around the double-parked car and eventually a larger vehicle like a delivery truck can't get by. The owner of the double-parked car has gone inside some building. The blocked truck starts honking as more and more cars pile up behind it. Eventually, many of the drivers of those blocked cars are leaning on their horns while the truck is now stuck between them and the double-parked car.

The owner of the double-parked car doesn't come out for a while, perhaps oblivious to the situation outside. During this time, many of the drivers are getting more and more angry. I've even seen the line of blocked cars backing up out of that street and going another way. But usually, they all just sit and wait and honk. Sometimes a few of them curse out their window at the owner of the double-parked car when he returns. A few times I've seen someone get out of their car and wait by the double-parked car to give the owner a piece of their mind.

-=-=-=-=-=-

When you feel angry, there is, indeed, a real urgency. But often the most urgent need is to take care of your anger itself rather than what you perceive as its cause. In our anger, we make so many hasty decisions. We say and do so many hurtful things only to regret them sooner or later. Sometimes, we make things even worse as we wrap our actions up in justifications, trying to shield ourselves from remorse. Often, when anger arises in us, it is not in response to an urgent threat. Rather than what is happening around us, the most destructive and dangerous element in the scene is our own anger burning inside of us.

We may feel that those responsible for our anger have to pay for what they've done, and only then can our anger settle down. But instead of focusing on any external cause, usually we can and should handle our anger by first working within ourselves. Through mindful breathing, we can come back to ourselves and slowly calm our mind and body. Then, when we feel more solid, we can look more deeply into our perception of what is going on. From there, we will be in the best position to address what needs addressing.

It helps to check in with our mind and body throughout the day. What is your breathing like right now? Do you feel any tension in your body, or your blood pressure climbing? How centered and balanced does your mind feel right now? Or how frantic? This is a look at the quality of your mind itself, rather than any individual thought it's producing. If we can recognize and embrace our anger with our mindfulness, we become more than just our anger. We will have many more options in how we respond than if we had just handed over the reins.

Often, the most compassionate thing we can do even for ourselves is to focus on cooling our anger rather than spending valuable time and energy lashing out. We've probably already seen the quality our actions towards others when our body or mind is distressed. Often, what we do in anger will at the very least not be helpful. Our actions may even escalate the situation, bringing more suffering. Sometimes just a quick check-in is eye-opening or jolting enough to shift our mental state. Other times, it is a good beginning but we need to stay with our breathing for some minutes or even longer as our anger cools off and we regain our center.

However long this takes, it is time well spent. If we deny our emotions and skip or rush through this, we can cause a lot of harm. Once we find ourselves and our balance again, then we can move forward with our full intelligence and patience. We'll have a much better shot at not making things worse and we'll be giving our best to improve the situation.

Diet

I step away from my computer to take a walk outside. I want the fresh air and maybe I can find some fresh perspective on my work. After strolling down the main street for a while I recall some great bakeries in the direction I'm headed. But I tell myself no, I had a big lunch not that long ago, I'm trying to lose some weight, and the last time I bought not one, but two pastries. As delicious as they were, I regretted almost every bite after the first. So this time, I tell myself no.

I'm enjoying the walk very much. It's beautiful outside and I'm grateful to be able to take this walk. I come to the first bakery. I just want to peek through the glass. I see they're out of what I usually get there, perfect, moving right along. I come to the second bakery. I like almost everything there. I go inside to have a closer look. I see some old favorites and some new things that look amazing. I have, on occasion, succeeded in popping into a bakery with intent to buy, even deciding what I would get, and while waiting in line, thought better of it and left empty handed.

Today, there was no line. I see two things I'd love to get but I at least decide that, no, I will only get one. I tell myself that I can always come back if, miraculously, I'm still hungry. Note that I'm not currently hungry at all, I just want my sugar fix. I choose a chocolate pudding tart with whipped cream on top. It's so big, I'm essentially getting two things. I tell them just to put it in a paper bag, I don't need a box. She reminds me that it has whipped cream on it, but I reply that I'm not carrying it that far. Actually, I have every intention of eating it just out of sight of the bakery staff. I could eat it there inside or at the benches immediately outside, but I'm starting to feel a bit ashamed of my plan to eat the whole thing. I at least don't want them to see me do it.

A few bites in, a familiar feeling of guilt arises. It occurs to me that I could stop right there. I don't need to take even a single bite more. This is a dangerous line of thought, so I immediately take another two bites. But everything about those bites confirms to me that this isn't what I want to be doing. I want to be enjoying my walk outside. I don't need this. "Why did I buy this thing, let alone start eating it, if I didn't want it?! What am I gonna do with it now, throw it out?! Waste it?..." I placed it back in the bag and dropped it in the trash can at the next corner.

Bushwhacking

To temporarily escape a cold New York City winter, I took a short vacation with a friend to St. Croix. This was four months after the category 5 Hurricane Maria had hit the island. We decided on St. Croix in the spur of the moment and had not done enough research to understand how hard life still was there. Even after four months, power had not been restored to large parts of the island. It was in fact only due to a computer error that our booking had gone through at all. The place we were staying was only hosting emergency service workers at that time. Even with all this, we met so many friendly people, and the natural beauty of the island still shone through. Each day we took a taxi ride to some new part of the island to explore on foot.

Near the end of the trip, I suggested we try to see the Annaly Bay Tide Pools. I made this suggestion purely based on pictures I found online that indicated that both the destination and the hike to get there would be very beautiful. Looking at a map, it seemed we would be able to drive right up to the trail we would be hiking, but the dirt roads near there were so bad still that our taxi got almost completely stuck twice. Perhaps our driver was as adventurous as we were or hoping for a large tip, because he still tried to get us quite close. But eventually he had to give up. We then had to decide whether to continue on foot from there to the trail, or to just go back with him.

The weather was great, we had driven a long way to get there, and we had no other plans for the day, so I wanted to give it a go. The driver asked how long we would be as he had to figure out whether to wait there or come back for us later. We settled on him picking us up four hours later. Already our plan carried significant risk as the meeting spot was a completely unmarked and unremarkable intersection within a maze of dirt roads. Our driver had confidence he would arrive back at the right spot at the right time. I don't know why I trusted that or why I trusted that my friend and I would get back there either. Especially as cell phone reception was essentially non-existent.

The taxi driver departed and we began walking. Soon after we hit the trail, things weren't going well for my friend. He hadn't anticipated the muddy and rough conditions we would face. He became increasingly frustrated as his shoes got ruined, he kept slipping, and as we had to keep climbing over and around uprooted trees and other debris blocking the trail. Eventually, at an abandoned Jeep we came across, he decided that he was done with all this. He said he wanted to just sit right where he was to rest and eventually he would head back to wait for the taxi driver.

There was still a lot of time left till the taxi would arrive and I was still feeling full of energy. There was also a precedent for this friend splitting off to head back during some of our previous long walks. But this was a long *hike*, not a walk, and in a remote place new to both of us. So, in one of the poorest decisions of my life, I suggested that I would press on to try and make the end of the trail, while he could either wait there or start hiking back.

As I pressed on, the trail became more and more overgrown. More and more often, I found myself unsure if I was even still on the trail. Although I had completely lost cell reception, my GPS was showing that I was slowly but surely getting closer to my goal. Looking at my watch, I still had time. Eventually I was entirely bushwhacking and I was getting continuously caught on brambles. My progress was slowing down considerably, I was out of water, and getting very tired. An earlier realization dawned on me anew that every step farther that I made was another I would have to retrace to get back. Soon I could finally hear the ocean waves hitting the shore and felt I was so close. I had come so far. I almost had the trophy. But, somehow, it finally hit me that I might have already gone too far.

I turned around and started bushwhacking back. After a certain point, I still hadn't hit easier trail but knew that I should have by then. I was feeling almost completely exhausted and knew that I needed to find the trail and stop bushwhacking soon. It hit me that I could die there. The forest was so thick that even if they sent a helicopter they wouldn't be able to see me. Then I thought about my friend. What would he and the taxi driver do when I didn't return? Would they possibly get lost as well trying to find me? Was my friend even able to find the meeting place for the taxi on his own? What a fool I had been! *I had to fix this now.* Based off GPS I picked a direction that I would certainly T into the trail eventually, there was no way to miss it. I pushed hard and by sheer luck I was soon back on easy trail, and trail that I remembered!

I finally made it back to the abandoned Jeep where I had left from my friend but there was no sign of him. He must have decided to head back on his own. At a certain point, I came to a fork in the trail. It took me a long minute to remember which way we had come from. Then I wondered if my friend got it right. I was getting more worried about him and I decided to call out for him a few times. Then I had a horrible thought. What if he was actually OK, but, upon hearing my calls, tried to find me and got lost? I decided I wouldn't call out for him again unless I was back at the meeting spot and didn't see him. I imagined having to explain to his mother how I was the cause of her son dying. He never goes on hikes, how could I split up from him?!

Eventually almost back at the meeting spot. I could see him! He was alive! We were both alive! We weren't even late. But would the taxi driver return? Would he remember where we agreed to meet? Would he avoid getting stuck? Still overjoyed and hugging my friend, I found out that he didn't share any of the concerns that I had carried. Seeing my confidence in the beginning, he assumed everything we did was a legitimate and safe enough thing to be doing. I had let him down. Why was it so important for me to finish another hike or bag one more beautiful vista?

There was still a little time left before we were supposed to meet the taxi driver. From the map on my phone, there was only one road that lead to the web of roads we were on. I suggested it was less risky if we waited at that road instead as he would have to drive by there to get to our meeting spot. I thought meeting him there would be fewer steps for him and there would be less chance of him making a wrong turn and missing us. While walking toward that road we saw him driving towards us.

-=-=-=-=-=-

Flowing with things doesn't mean not steering or changing anything. And it certainly doesn't include closing our eyes to what we feel, what we realize, or what's in front of us. No matter how out of line it is with our current course. We can open our eyes and use our full intelligence to understand what is happening right now. Then we'll know what needs to happen next and what doesn't. We don't have to be bound by previous plans or conclusions formed in moments past. What matters is: what does *this* moment call for?

7 | New Beginnings

"Your parents did the best they could with what they had."

That's what a therapist said to me about ten years ago. By that point, she had an understanding of my past from our conversations, and from the following exercise that she gave me: Write down three of your most painful memories. Read them into a tape recorder. Listen to them until you can see them plainly as events that happened; until you can acknowledge and accept that they happened…

"My mom and dad were in the kitchen. I was seven and my brother was five. She was screaming at my dad while crying and holding a knife, the blade's edge against her skin. My brother and I had come over to see what the screaming was about. My brother, tears streaming down his face, cried out 'Momma, I'm sorry.' My dad turned to me and said, 'At least your brother knows what he should say.' I couldn't speak."

My eyes tear up thinking about it. My brother was five, barely older than my daughter is now. I absolutely could not imagine subjecting her to any part of that scene. She's affected whenever her mom is even just sad. This scene would shatter her.

I relived that event, and two others, many times as I wrote them down and as I listened to my recorded voice reading them. None of them could I write out completely in one go. For one in particular, I stabbed my notebook again and again with my pen. Soon, I was using the pen to claw out the paper, violently revolting against what had happened all those years ago. I couldn't look at it. It hurt too much. But I stayed with it, and gradually, I could look at it. Over time, something changed as I relived those memories. I wasn't worthless or unlovable, even while being treated as if I were. I had logically known that, but now I could feel it.

Raw pain fell away, leaving a deep sadness and disappointment. I was damn sure that my parents *didn't* "do the best they could." I wasn't interested in what they had to work with; they had failed. They had built all around me the very things that parents are supposed to shield their children from. That *they* were supposed to shield *me* from.

About five years ago, I had a dream in which my dad and I were standing alone in a room. He started to take a swing at me, but I knocked him down first and jumped on top of him. Pinning him to the ground, my hands around his throat, I yelled, "No. We're done with this." I got up as he still lay there, stunned.

Though I had lived through long periods of hating him and trying to block him from my memory, in this dream, I wasn't trying to hurt him. I wanted all of the senseless suffering to stop, *now*.

How did everything go so wrong in my family growing up? My dad's doctors never concluded what caused his neurological symptoms. Though they considered multiple sclerosis and Lyme disease (eventually ruling both out), the answer would not explain his behavior, which had been prevalent for many, many years.

I know that our relationship evolved over time. When I was very little, I was his "little monkey" and he never hit me. When he hit me for the first time, I believe it shocked him as much as it did me.

I do have a few good memories of my dad. I was probably around six the first time he took me to the auto repair shop he worked at. He was proud of the questions I asked him, joking that they were better than the ones from his coworker. He was also proud of me one morning when he was came to my school for a bagel breakfast, given to the families of high achieving students. There was a nice radio-controlled car he bought for me one birthday. I loved when occasionally, I found a way onto his good side, and he'd take me to a big open parking lot to race that RC car around. Once, we worked together on a school project, a medieval style shield crafted out of wood. There was the time he found me when I got lost during a camping trip.

But that's it. Out of all my memories of him, there are no other moments I can look back on positively. We didn't spend much time doing things together. I hardly ever spoke to him unless he spoke to me; and he only spoke to me if I had done something wrong.

I can't even picture his face; I had learned to never look him in the eye.

"I'm much nicer to you than my father was to us growing up. He would throw plates at us. Knocked out one of my sister's teeth." I believe that's true. I remember being hungry before meals and being grateful for food. But I don't remember any sense of relaxation, joy, or connection. I imagine he felt the same lack in the meals he had with his family growing up, and later in the meals he had with us.

My mom told me a few things about him. His own dad had died when he was only fifteen, after which he dropped out of high school to start working and help support his family. I know that he buried his own dreams for the future with that decision. He was embarrassed of his family and his living conditions. So much so that he refused to show my mom where he lived until shortly before they got married. Ironically, we all ended up living in the poorly converted basement of that same house. He never got to move on.

He had to be in absolute control of the people around him. During a disagreement with my mom, he disconnected the spark plug wires in her car so that she wouldn't be able to drive away. She once told me that my dad got her pregnant on the advice of his buddies at work, to "keep her busy."

The last time I talked to my dad was through that locked door to the upstairs. He said, "I don't hate your grandmother anymore; she's a good person. I was also wrong about your brother, he just sees things differently." He told me this short story. "I showed your brother four letters on a sheet of paper —d, b, q, and p—and asked him what they were. He said they were all the same, and I thought 'Oh God, he's really screwed up.' Then he told me that they are all a circle on a stick and I understood. The public school wanted him in a special program to help him. I figured no son of mine is going to be put in a special program. That's why I pulled him out and put him in private school. I shouldn't have done that."

I was shocked to hear honest regrets from him.

There's so much I don't know about my dad. How deeply did he reflect on his life before he fell mentally ill, or during the long hours alone upstairs afterward? Was there anything that he wished he could change? If so, how hard did he try, or did he not even feel capable of change?

Maybe he felt this was just who he was, or that all the hard times were brought on by everyone else's mistakes. Did anyone ever talk to him about emotions? I don't know if he ever asked for help. I can only guess how abusive his dad was to him, and how it affected him. I'll never know what part, if any, brain chemical imbalances, drugs, and alcohol played.

I slowly learned to forgive my dad, and separately my mom, years ago. But it wasn't until I started seriously working with and pulling together the ideas in this book, that I ceased blaming them for what happened. I see now, that on one level, they were in the same situation all of us are. From a confluence of causes, certain thoughts and feelings came up for them. And thoughts and feelings in opposition to those either didn't come up, or didn't resonate. My parents did the best they could with what they had. Despite trying, I'll never know most of the story. If my dad was torn at times, I didn't have any window into that. I only knew the words and actions he sent out into the world. And felt the absence of the ones he didn't. It's just sad that *any of us* had to live through that.

That's all now part of the background of my own actions. I accept that, and try my best to work with it skillfully.

I had often heard that we should see ourselves as a continuation of our parents. For most of my life, the thought that I could be a continuation of my father filled me with disgust. I hoped with all my being that there was nothing of him in me. But one morning, two years ago, I realized that being a continuation of my dad is important, even something to be happy about. For if I am his continuation, then through me, he can have a second chance. He can learn how to be loving and compassionate. He can learn to ride the waves of emotion without drowning in them, and without pulling others under with him. He can understand. These thoughts still make me smile.

I feel very lucky that several meditation and mindfulness practices *felt* right to me early on. This feeling motivated me to keep reading and trying new things. Eventually, they became more than just tools to find calm or to work through a particular issue. They had become, for me, a way of approaching life. Along the way, I believe I've come to understand a little about how our mind works. How that understanding conflicts with how we typically hold people accountable, and how we try to change those people, forms the inspiration for this book.

I still have a lot of inner work to do, but that keeps things interesting. I am grateful for all the help I've received and all the valuable insights that people have made the effort to share. Without them, my life would not be the same. I know that the many moments of tranquility, wonder, and happiness that I find in my days would be much rarer. And I would not have the same loving relationships that I do with my wife and daughter.

8 | Tools

In this book I'm asking you to make a shift in your thinking and change deep-rooted habits. Even if you are committed to doing so, this is no small task. I included exercises in chapter 3 to shine a light on our situation and provide motivation to make this shift. In this chapter I offer a collection of exercises as tools to further motivate and support your effort. Some of these exercises strengthen mindfulness of your thoughts and feelings. Others point to new perspectives on your experiences.

The ideas and traditions I've borrowed from in writing this book have been around for a long time. My hope is that my presentation of them here will be helpful. I've included a reading list at the end of this book if you're interested in reading further.

Whichever tools you choose, it's crucial that you use them in service of connecting more authentically with your experiences and your life. If you attempt to spiritually bypass your difficulties, you will make things worse. If you deny your emotions, they will still influence your actions. You may blow up at others unexpectedly, blaming them, without understanding yourself. You may spill your suffering onto others since you are not addressing it within yourself. The numbness and distance you'll have to maintain to keep your sadness at bay will keep some of your joy at bay as well.

This is not to say you shouldn't carve out moments of peace to nourish yourself, even in the midst of a storm. Clearing your mind to rejuvenate yourself and maybe gain perspective and balance can be essential at times. But eventually, you have to come back to address what you can and begin accepting what you can't.

Another word of caution: concepts and ideas are themselves just tools. They can be used skillfully or, if applied at the wrong time, can cause a lot of trouble. Often, our view is skewed or incomplete and we need to look at things through the lens of a very different idea. This can bring us balance as it tips us back towards center. Just be careful not to go too far past center in some new direction. One perspective isn't absolutely better or higher than another. However, certain perspectives may be more useful in certain situations.

When working with seemingly opposing viewpoints, sometimes you need to find a balance. Other times one of them is more appropriate in a given moment. In some cases they both apply at the same time. For example, maintaining either too much self-concern or not enough both often end badly. In this case finding the balance is most helpful. However, specific situations may call for temporarily shifting your concern towards one extreme or the other. In other cases, it may be clear that concern for self and other are interdependent or one in the same.

Note that any given way of talking about something can only capture some narrow aspect of it, never the full reality of the thing. New perspectives gained from these exercises complement, rather than replace, how you already see things.

So please, do all you can to remain flexible and balanced in your ideas. With that said, below are some exercises to try. Any technique, duration, setting, or frequency mentioned is just an initial suggestion; feel free to modify them as you see fit. Try them out in different situations and maybe a few will click with you. I hope you have fun with some of them. However, do not attempt any of these exercises that you cannot perform safely. So if you're game, let's begin.

Fresh Eyes

When I go somewhere that I've never been before I automatically start paying more attention. I notice the smaller details of things that I normally tune out or walk right past; things become novel. This effect is exaggerated for me if I'm on vacation somewhere new. Sometimes we shift into this frame of mind when we visit places designed for us to notice things, such as a museum, zoo, or botanic garden. However, we can intentionally shift into this frame of mind at any time.

This isn't about ignoring or forgetting what you know, including which objects and actions are potentially dangerous, harmful, or costly. However you can still intentionally aim to be curious about something as if experiencing it for the first time. In doing so, you may learn some new things and remember old things you've long since forgotten. Find the pleasant or interesting aspects of things you've learned to tune out of your awareness. Try to combine the wisdom of an adult with the curiosity of a child. Coming to a place where things are understood yet not taken for granted, you may, at least for a moment, feel a sense of wonder.

Run your fingers over things you've walked right past for years: bushes, brick walls, tree bark, soil, a certain piece of furniture, a fence. Pick up something for no other reason than to feel the weight of it in your hand. Turn off your TV and music and focus on the sounds around you: your breathing, traffic, distant conversation, birds, wind, footsteps, electrical hum, and any motor sounds. Tap objects with your knuckles or scratch them with your fingernails to hear what sound is released. Look around and see the patterns in leaves, texture on the ground, shadows, the shine off objects, the way people, animals, and things blown by the wind move. Consider the universe of things around you. Isn't there something remarkable about it? Can you enjoy sitting in the car even in traffic? Can you view a pigeon or squirrel as an exotic animal? Can you walk down the block and look at the plants as if you're strolling through a botanical garden?

Balance

Stand barefoot on one or two feet depending on your ability. Tip your body forward from your ankles as far as you can. Can you go a little further? Try this a few times while trying to catch a few of the following: the sensation of being almost too far off balance; the thoughts around needing to not go any further; what different parts of your body do in response including your feet, core, and arms.

Try it again while leaning your body backward from your ankles. If you're so inclined, there are many yoga poses you can try balancing with as well. (For example, you can try with boat pose. Feel free to modify it by having your knees bent and feet closer to your center so it requires less core strength. However, with boat pose, make sure you're balancing entirely on your buttocks.) Try shifting your balance different ways and watch how your body responds. Which body movements do you feel in control of? Which are just "happening"? Deeply investigate this distinction.

Just Sitting

Find somewhere you can sit and watch the world go by. This could be in front of your home, at a park, at the mall or wherever you like. For the most part, just sit there and watch what your mind does. Depending on your frame of mind and what pops up, you may find it funny, ridiculous, amazing, or sometimes sad.

Once while sitting in front of my home, I noticed a Jeep Wrangler parked on the street. My eyes caught the "Sahara" emblem on it. "A trip to the Sahara sounds amazing," I thought. "But then there would be all equipment I'd only use once. And were there mosquitoes there? But to really experience the feeling of the Sahara, the way it is in the movies, would mean being lost and short on water. Is there a way to experience that and not die? If only I could just be there for a few minutes and then pop right back home... Ha! What am I doing? Is this why I came out here?"

Labels

Is waiting in line or in traffic a moment to catch your breath or an annoyance? Take notice of the process by which you frame what you encounter. Often once we categorize someone we're no longer seeing them, even when they're standing right in front of us. Watch the judgments and labels you apply as you move through your day. Does anything or anyone escape our habit of judging and labeling? To what degree are we reacting to our labels instead of what is actually there?

Routine

If any part of your day has become extremely routine, observe it closely for a few days. For example: the sequence and details of how you walk up the stairs, get your keys out of your pocket, and unlock and open the door to your home each day after work. Observe your thoughts and phrases in certain recurring situations. Don't force it too soon, maybe it will take a week. But eventually your actions may play out in front of you like a movie. Down the line, see what your observations do and do not change about how things play out.

Impermanence

Feel the impermanence of everything you see, everything you are experiencing. For example, walk down the block and consider the very sidewalk you're walking on. Vividly imagine how the seasons, with their leaves, rain, snow and sunshine have played across it through the years. See far enough into the past that the concrete wasn't even poured yet. There may have been a dirt or gravel road. Further back a forest, desert or swamp. Imagine the future of this sidewalk you now stand on. As the years fly by, all the buildings around will shift and change. Far enough in the future there may not be anyone living in the area at all.

Try this with other important things in your life as well. This could be your home, the roads or trains you use to get to work, or a grocery store. Try a version of this that focuses on the people in your life, including yourself. Consider the uniqueness of this present moment.

Lines

See the lines we draw with our mind to be of our own creation rather than determined by external reality. Start with lines that most clearly seem to be by convention or for convenience rather than a real separation existing. Take for example lines of latitude or longitude or other lines on a map. Many times there is nothing notable or different about the land or water on either side of the line. Consider where we draw the line between certain parts of the human body. Is there a hard line separating them or do the parts flow and blend into each other?

Consider the separation we draw between a plant and its environment. Right where we draw the line between the plant and its soil there are exchanges of nutrients just as complex as those that occur within the plant itself. Imagine molecules and atoms as they move across these lines we've drawn. At an atomic scale is there any significance to these lines?

Most objects we perceive as solid and motionless are in reality composed of countless atoms in constant motion and they allow radio waves and magnetic fields to pass right through them. Your cell phone still rings from radio signals it receives even when buried in your pocket or bag. A solid glass window lets light pass right through. How sure are we of the boundaries we've defined?

Everything around and within you is one continuous sea of matter and energy. *You* slice it up into separate objects through your perception of it. You group together some volume of matter, give it a name, and treat it a certain way. In this way, you create or give reality to everything around you, including yourself. Imagine a world, including oceans, mountains, fields, clouds, all manner of terrain and weather, but without even a single living thing around to observe, name, judge or experience any part of it. Does a falling tree make a sound if no one is around to hear it? Does a world exist if no one experiences it?

Role

You're playing a role in a game. But for the game to have any real value, you can't stand aloof from it. You need to get into the role *while* understanding it as a role you're playing. From this wider perspective, see in what new ways you can play around with your role and which moments you choose to take seriously. You may find new opportunities to create joy.

Scales

All the scales you measure against are a creation. Imagine your scales of big/small, quiet/loud, low/high, and fast/slow. Try this from the perspective of someone much older or younger; someone much richer or poorer. Try this from the perspective of a bug, a whale, or a bird. Your current scales may suit your life and goals. But imagine radically different viewpoints deeply enough to temporarily experience them as equally or even more valid.

Formations

Blink as rapidly as you can comfortably sustain and look around. You can try this sitting down or walking around in a safe area. Try to see each thing in front of you as an instantaneous and momentary formation, snapping into place. Each thing is newly formed in each moment out of whatever energy is there. But how it forms is dependent on all the conditions surrounding it, including everything else snapping into place. When you're ready, try seeing yourself, your thoughts, and other people also as momentary formations. Now see this without blinking.

When the conditions in one moment are close enough to the conditions of the previous moment, a given formation, for example a given person, may seem the same in both moments. There is continuity. But what about when the conditions change significantly in the next moment? Many life-changing things can happen in an instant, both grave and miraculous. A person may die or become seriously injured; or a doctor may restart their heart. A normally cheerful person can lose someone and become depressed for a long time, or become deeply scarred and bitter from a single event. Miraculously, a person who has been angry for many years, may suddenly see things a different way, and their personality and life are transformed. Consider the times one's identity is changed in an instant, including becoming a parent or losing a job they've had most of their adult life.

Each new moment will always contain some conditions similar to the previous, so there will always be some sense of continuity. But each new moment will also always be unique and contain new conditions, which open the door to new possibilities. We can tap into our full potential by loosening our grasp on the past and our demand for continuity.

Actions

When an actor is performing an action on an object; the actor, the action, and the object are one. Each of the three is dependent on and shaped by the other two.

Consider the act of seeing. Seeing is necessarily *someone* seeing *something*. The action is shaped by the actor and the object. For example, "you seeing a tree" is the coming together of at least your eyes, your mind, and that tree. You need the light from the sun bouncing off the tree and into your eyes. Your mind needs to be paying attention, and your memory and understanding of trees is required for you to focus on the image and see it *as a tree*. A newborn may see the same patterns of light and color but won't be able to conceptualize it as a tree. Your mental state and predispositions influence whether you see the tree as beautiful or in some other light, and even whether you notice the tree at all. How the action plays out and its total effect, what the action truly is, is dependent on both the actor and the object.

The actor is also shaped by the action and the object. Seeing something makes an impression on your mind, leading to thoughts, decisions and further actions. What is seen can have emotional impact. It also plants a memory to be recalled or dreamed about later. It may provide inspiration for handling future circumstances. How you perform the action is guided and shaped by the object. When seeing, the object can pull you into looking closer or push you to look away. Certain details may command your attention. If you become fully absorbed in observing the object it becomes more present to you than your own body and for a time your mind is one with the object. You are the object.

In many cases it is clear how the object is affected by the action. However, even with a passive action like seeing, an object like a tree can be transformed. How a tree is seen changes its place in the universe, and its fate. A tree seen as a work of art or a source of fruit or refreshing shade may be treasured and protected. Seen in another light, a tree may be seen as nuisance, its roots pushing up and damaging a sidewalk, or its branches getting too close a building or power lines, or it may drop smelly fruit or sticky pollen that must be dealt with. In a way, a tree has become firewood as soon as it as seen as such, well before being cut down.

Looking deeper, we find that there's a whole universe of things that bring into being, sustain, and give the context for *you-seeing-that-tree*. If any of it is missing or altered there is no longer the same "you seeing that tree". Try to notice and respect this interdependence and unity of actor, action, and object for actions you notice and respond to. This unity applies to outward actions as much as an inward action like thinking.

Shifting Focus

For many of us, our mental focus is usually on the dialogue in our minds, the internal chattering about our experience, instead of the experience itself. It should be noted that in this case your experience becomes your mind's chattering. This exercise is about shifting your focus to your immediate physical experience. However it usually doesn't work to tell oneself not to focus on a given thing as then that directive (including the object) becomes the focus. Instead an alternate focus needs to be provided.

Choose a sense such as hearing, sight, or touch to use as an anchor to your experience. I found for myself hearing works well as this anchor. Whenever you notice your focus has drifted from your immediate physical experience, gently and immediately bring it back to your anchor. Remember that having an internal conversation about coming back is *not* the same as actually coming back.

Our anchor within a given sense can be general or specific. When I choose my sense of touch, I usually anchor to the feeling of my breath moving or the feeling of my feet pressing off the ground as I walk. But I could instead continually shift among any of my bodily sensations.

The intention with this exercise is to bring balance back to our focus. Our internal dialogue can produce valuable results, but our experience needs to also include the reality in front of us. Otherwise that internal dialogue will be mostly about itself.

Future

Explore how the present moment contains the future. As you perform various actions, imagine your future self interacting with the result. For example, when you take your shoes off imagine your future self having to deal with where and how you have placed them.

We can only imagine the future and we only have a certain level of influence over it. But even within those constraints, we can have fun with the future and notice some interesting things.

Closing

Thank you for sticking with me to the end. Writing this book has been an emotional journey for me. I hope that reading this book helps you as much as writing it has helped me.

I believe we've mislaid our blame, our anger, and our punishments for too long. We need to stop, and we should help each other to stop. This isn't about giving up or becoming passive. I'm asking that we proactively look deeply at our shared human experience and then respond with our full intelligence and capacity. This will take a sustained commitment on our part.

We have to be willing to look into ourselves and others even in the presence of pain and anger. We have to keep looking with an open mind even as harsh judgment arises within us. Most likely we will often still fall short, but that's all part of it as well. Please don't wait for the next challenging situation. By looking into even our most mundane moments, we can build up the right habits as well as our reserve of strength and understanding.

Our inner and outer worlds could be such a friendlier place to live. If we look deeply and persist in our efforts, we may not need to punish anymore.

Reading List

Watts, Alan. *The Book: On the Taboo Against Knowing Who You Are*. Vintage Books, 1972.

Hanh, Thich Nhat. *Anger: Wisdom for Cooling the Flames*. Riverhead Books, 2002.

Chodron, Pema, et al. *Taking the Leap: Freeing Ourselves from Old Habits and Fears*. Shambhala, 2010.

Salzberg, Sharon. *Lovingkindness: The Revolutionary Art of Happiness*. Shambhala, 2002.

Hanh, Thich Nhat. *The Art of Living: Peace and Freedom in the Here and Now*. HarperOne, 2017.

Watts, Alan, and Al Chung-Liang Huang. *Tao: The Watercourse Way*. Pantheon Books, 1975.

Watts, Alan, and Mark Watts. *Still the Mind: An Introduction to Meditation*. New World Library, 2002.

Kabat-Zinn, Jon, and University of Massachusetts Medical Center/Worcester. Stress Reduction Clinic. *Full Catastrophe Living: Using the Wisdom of Your Body and Mind to Face Stress, Pain, and Illness*. Delta Trade Paperbacks, 1991.

Reps, Paul, and Nyogen Senzaki. *Zen Flesh, Zen Bones: A Collection of Zen and Pre-Zen Writings*. Paperback with Flaps, Tuttle Publishing, 1998.

Suzuki, Shunryu, et al. *Not Always So: Practicing the True Spirit of Zen*. HarperCollins, 2003.

Saint-Exupéry, Antoine de, et al. *The Little Prince*. Harcourt, 2000.

$0 = 1 = \infty$

Don't be a jerk.

everything changes

Treat all things with gratitude and care.

Everything is a borrow.

"I'm sorry."

"Excuse me."

This is it!

www.ingramcontent.com/pod-product-compliance
Lightning Source LLC
Chambersburg PA
CBHW030331080526
44584CB00012B/815